Contents

Some words are shown in bold, **like this**. You can find out what they mean by looking in the Glossary.

Roll up! Roll up!

Take a trip to the circus. You'll be amazed by the **acrobats** and **trapeze** artists flying high above your head. With a little bit of practice, you could amaze your friends with your own circus skills.

Don't Try This at Home!

C---s

Tricks

Nick Hunter

Raintree is an imprint of Capstone Global Library
Limited, a company incorporated in England and Wales
having its registered office at 7 Pilgrim Street, London,
EC4V 6LB – Registered company number: 6695582

To contact Raintree please phone 0845 6044371,
fax + 44 (0) 1865 312263, or email myorders@
raintreepublishers.co.uk. Customers from outside the
UK please telephone +44 1865 312262.

Edited by Rebecca Rissman, Daniel Nunn,
  and Adrian Vigliano
Designed by Cynthia Della-Rovere
Picture research by Elizabeth Alexander
Production by Alison Parsons
Originated by Capstone Global Library Ltd
Printed and bound in China by China Translation
  and Printing Services Ltd

ISBN 978 1 406 25101 2 (hardback)
16 15 14 13 12
10 9 8 7 6 5 4 3 2 1

ISBN 978 1 406 25108 1 (paperback)
17 16 15 14 13
10 9 8 7 6 5 4 3 2 1

British Library Cataloguing in Publication Data
Hunter, Nick.
Silly circus tricks. -- (Try this at home!)
791.3-dc23
A full catalogue record for this book is available from
the British Library.

Acknowledgements
We would like to thank the following for permission
to reproduce photographs: Alamy p. 17 (© maxim.
photoshelter.com); © Capstone Publishers pp. 7, 8, 9
t, 9 b, 10, 11, 12, 13 t, 13 b, 14, 15 t, 15 b, 16, 19
t, 19 b, 20 t, 21, 20 b, 22 t, 22 b, 23 t, 23 b, 26, 27
t, 27 b, 28, 29 (Karon Dubke); Getty Images pp. 5
(William West/AFP), 18 (Abdelhak Senna/AFP), 24
(Hannes Magerstaedt), 25 (Fotosearch); Shutterstock
pp. 4 (© Hung Chung Chih), 6 (© michaeljung).
Design features reproduced with the permission of
Shutterstock (© Christophe Boisson), (© Merve Poray),
(© Nicemonkey).

Cover photograph of a young woman juggling
reproduced with permission of Corbis (© Ocean).

Every effort has been made to contact copyright holders
of material reproduced in this book. Any omissions will
be rectified in subsequent printings if notice is given to
the publisher.

All the internet addresses (URLs) given in this book
were valid at the time of going to press. However, due to
the dynamic nature of the internet, some addresses may
have changed, or sites may have changed or ceased to
exist since publication. While the author and publisher
regret any inconvenience this may cause readers, no
responsibility for any such changes can be accepted by
either the author or the publisher.

Bloomington, Chicago, Mankato, Oxford

Big-top tip

Many circus tricks are highly dangerous and should only be performed by trained circus stars.

Amazing acrobats

Acrobats make difficult and dangerous tricks look simple. If you want to be like them, it's important to stay safe when trying any new move. Check that you have something soft to land on.

A handstand is a great first move for a young acrobat.

Big-top tip

Make sure you **warm up** and stretch your **muscles** before trying any tricks. You don't want to pull a muscle when you're upside down.

The handstand

STEP 1

Start by kneeling at the wall. Put your hands flat on the floor about 30 centimetres (12 inches) from the wall.

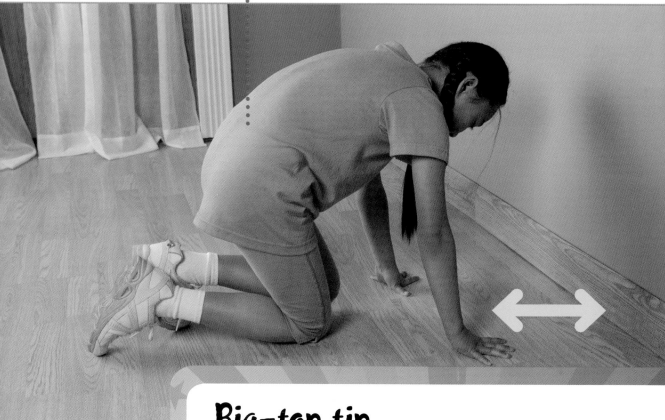

Big-top tip

Ask a friend to help you keep your legs straight and balance.

STEP 2

Straighten your legs to raise your hips into the air. Then kick one leg straight into the air until it's upright or resting on the wall.

STEP 3

Push your other leg into the air and point your toes. With practice, you'll be able to balance without the wall and even walk on your hands like a real circus **acrobat**.

Jazzy juggling

Level of difficulty:
Medium ⭐

STEP 1

Have you seen **jugglers** catching knives or even burning torches? Leave that to the experts. The best way to start is with just one ball.

Practise throwing the ball from one hand to the other. After a while, you should be able to catch it without even looking.

Big-top tip

Safety tips for first-time jugglers:

- Juggle with things that won't break (unlike this young juggler!).
- Clear some space so you don't knock things over.

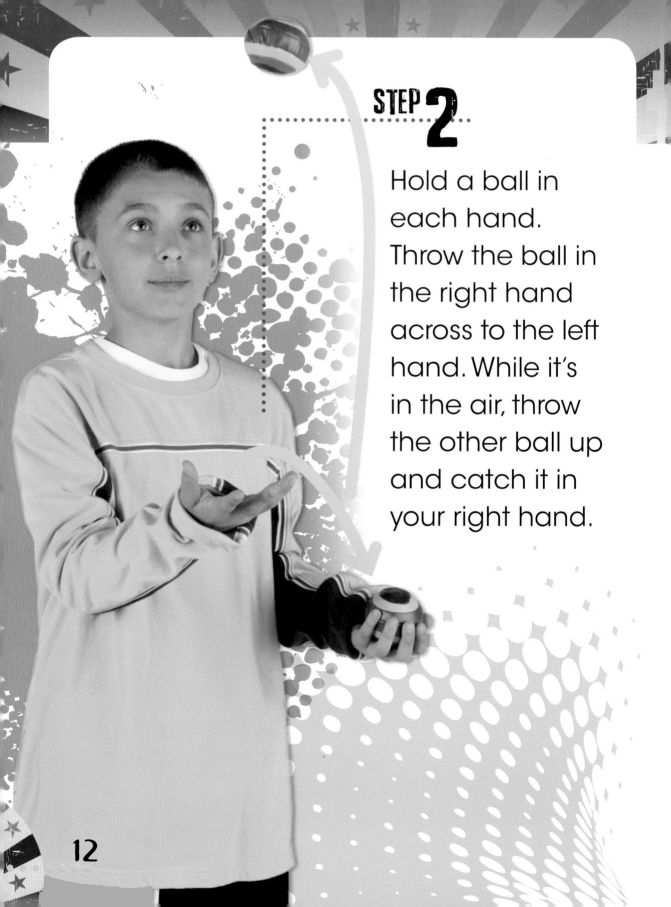

STEP 2

Hold a ball in each hand. Throw the ball in the right hand across to the left hand. While it's in the air, throw the other ball up and catch it in your right hand.

12

 **STEP 3**

When you can juggle easily with two balls, add another one. Throw and catch them in order as before. You'll have to be quick, as one ball will always be in the air.

Big-top tip

Don't throw the balls too high. This will make it more difficult to catch them.

Stilt crazy

Level of difficulty:
Medium

STEP **1**

How would you
like to tower
above your
friends? You can
start stilt walking
with simple
wooden **stilts**.

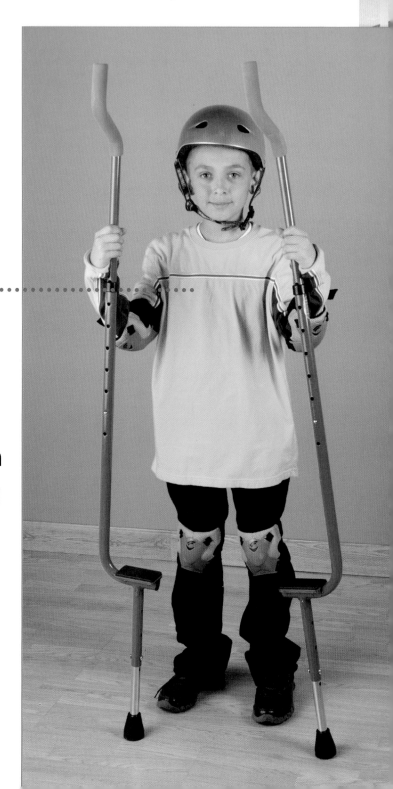

STEP 2

Your first challenge is standing up on stilts. It's easier to stand up if you start by sitting on a high seat, such as a stool or table.

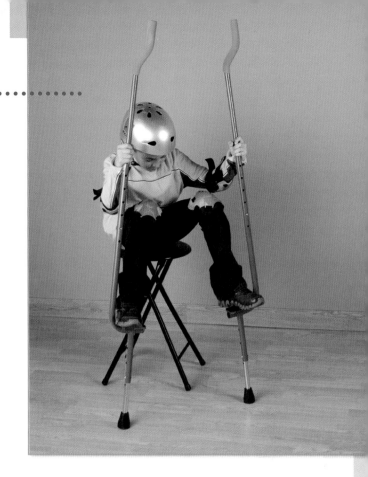

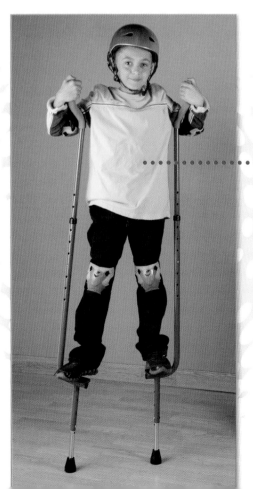

STEP 3

Once you're upright, stand as straight as you possibly can.

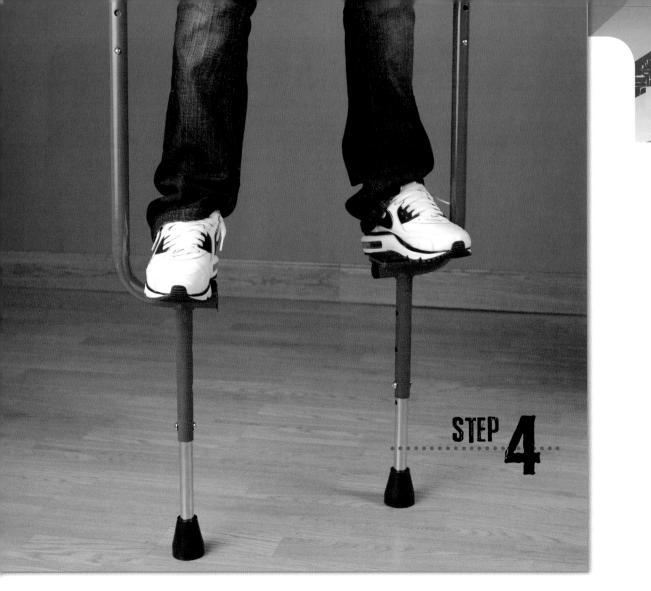

Practise marching on the spot with your
stilts. Keep a wall or rope near by to hold
on to. Once you know you can keep
your balance, try letting go. You can also
upgrade to circus stilts that you strap
onto your legs.

The circus is now just a few very big steps away.

Big-top tip

Make sure you wear gear that will protect you if you fall over, such as:

- a cycle helmet
- knee pads
- elbow pads or a padded jacket.

Walking a tightrope

Walking the high wire is an amazing circus act. It looks impossible. But with a lot of hard work, you can do it.

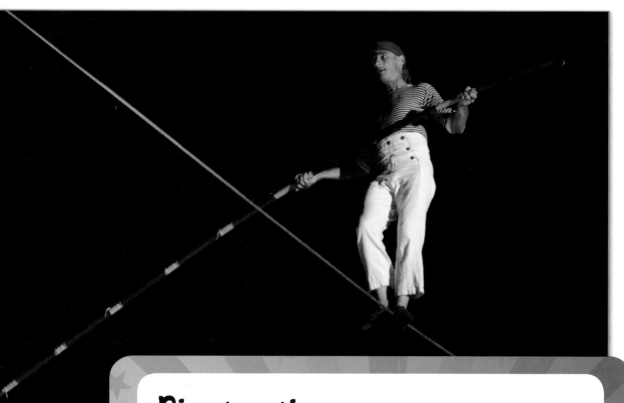

Big-top tip

If you want to master this difficult trick, you'll have to put in hours of practice.

STEP 1

Tightrope walking is all about balance. Practise standing very straight on one leg. Then try doing it with your eyes closed.

STEP 2

Next, practise walking along a line on the ground. Try to keep your weight on the balls of your feet. Turn around without falling off the line.

STEP 3

Now that you've got your balance, you can try standing on a slack rope. Bare feet will help you grip the rope.

STEP 4

First, put one foot on the rope and try to stand for as long as possible. Start from the middle of the rope.

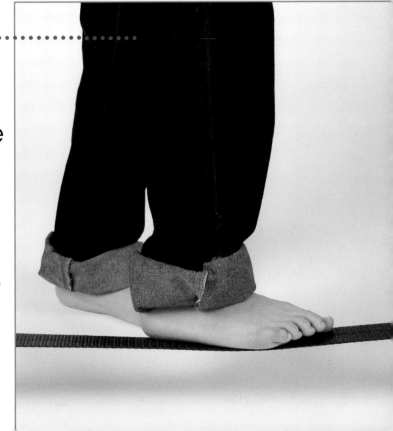

Keep your leg bent and point your foot along the rope. Using your other leg and spreading your arms will help you to balance.

Big-top tip

Start with a short rope close to the ground and a friend to help, so you won't end up with too many bruises.

STEP 6

If you can balance for several seconds, you're ready to try walking. Try placing your other foot on the wire in front of your standing foot.

STEP 7

Your weight usually goes onto your front foot. On a rope, keep your weight on the back foot as you put your front foot down.

When you get really good, you can turn around by placing your front foot across the rope. Twist around it so your back foot is facing the opposite way.

Big-top tip

If a friend sits on the rope, it will not move as much.

Clowning around

It wouldn't be a circus without the clowns. It may look like they're just messing around, but clowns need skills to make people laugh and do clever tricks.

Mad hair or a wacky wig

Painted face and a big red nose

The first thing you need is the right costume.

Brightly coloured clothes that are too big

Great big flappy shoes

Big-top tip
Don't forget funny **props**, like a plastic flower that squirts water.

Forward roll

Use the tricks you've already learnt and add new ones. A simple **forward roll** in a clown costume will have your audience laughing.

STEP 1

Lean towards the ground. You could pretend you're tying your shoelace. Put your hands on the floor and curve your back.

STEP 2

Push with
your legs, so
that your weight
carries your legs
over your head.

STEP 3

Roll over, keeping
your back
curved, and
stand up again.

Showtime!

Now that you know the tricks, you can really put on a show. Give yourself a silly name and find some great, sparkly clothes. Get your friends involved and pretend to be the **ringmaster**.

Big-top tip

Start your show with some easier tricks. You can build up to the most difficult and exciting acts, such as **tightrope** walking.

Glossary

acrobat someone who performs gymnastic tricks such as handstands and somersaults

forward roll trick in which a person rolls head over heels

juggler performer who can throw and catch several objects at once

muscle body part that makes your body move

prop object used as part of a show or circus act

ringmaster person who introduces the acts at a circus and runs the show

stilts leg extensions made of wood or other material

tightrope rope or wire fixed between two points above the ground and pulled tight

trapeze narrow platform or swing high above the ground in a circus

warm up exercise to make sure your body is prepared for action and to prevent injuries

Find out more

Books

Contortionists and Cannons: An Acrobatic Look at the Circus (Culture in Action), Marc Tyler Nobleman (Raintree, 2010)

The Usborne Book of Juggling, Clive Gifford (Usborne, 2009)

Who Walks the Tightrope? Working at a Circus (Wild Work), Mary Meinking (Raintree, 2010)

Websites

www.wgbh.org/articles/-777
This site features video tips from real circus performers.

www.circusarts.org.uk
This site features lots of information about circuses, where you can see them, and how you can improve your circus skills.

Index